BUILT TO LAST

What I've Learned, What I'm Learning, and What I Don't Know Yet About Marriage

Kevin Horton

Published independently.

First Edition

ISBN: 979-8-9951044-3-8

Cover design & Interior formatting: Mehrab Meraj

Printed in the United States of America

To my wife,

Thank you for building this life with me. The journey has been better than I ever imagined, and I'm grateful every day that I get to walk through it with you.

To my parents and my in-laws,

Thank you for showing us what a strong, lasting marriage looks like. Your example has meant more than you probably realize.

Contents

Introduction
Marriage Looks Different Than I Expected.....................................09

Part I
What I've Learned...**15**

Chapter 1
Respect Is the Foundation 17

Chapter 2
Out-Serve Each Other...25

Chapter 3
Just Say It...31

Chapter 4
Sacrifice Is Required 37

Chapter 5
Protect the Marriage...45

Chapter 6
Be Intentional 53

Chapter 7
Your Marriage Sets the Tone for the Family.......................61

A Season of Continued Learning

Part II
What I'm Learning..**67**

Chapter 8
Marriage Evolves Over Time 69

Chapter 9
People Experience Love and Respect Differently 75

Chapter 10
Balancing Work, Marriage, and Family 81

Chapter 11
Gratitude Strengthens a Marriage 87

Looking Ahead

Part III
What I Don't Know Yet **93**

Chapter 12
Marriage Through the Teenage Years 95

Chapter 13
The Empty Nest 101

Chapter 14
Growing Old Together 107

Closing Reflection **111**

About the Author **117**

Other Books by Kevin Horton **119**

Marriage Looks Different Than I Expected

My wife and I dated and were engaged for almost five years before we got married. By the time our wedding day arrived, marriage didn't feel like stepping into something completely unknown. In many ways, we had already begun building a life together.

We even bought a house together before we were married. That decision might not have been traditional by every standard, but it meant we were already experiencing some of the responsibilities and rhythms that come with building a household. We had learned how to make decisions together, how to handle stress, and how to move through life side by side.

Both of our parents also set strong examples of marriage. We saw relationships that were steady, respectful, and committed over the long haul. We also saw other relationships that struggled. Even if we didn't fully understand it at the time, those examples helped shape our expectations.

One thing that has always been unique about our relationship is that we have never broken up. From the time we started dating until now, we've never gone through the cycle that seems common in many relationships— breaking up, getting back together, and repeating the process.

That doesn't mean everything has always been easy.

It means that from early on, we both recognized that we had something real.

When people ask when I knew she was the person I wanted to marry, the truth is there wasn't one dramatic moment. We started dating in the summer. By the end of that year I already had an engagement ring, and by the following spring we were engaged.

From the outside it might have seemed fast, but it never felt rushed.

There wasn't one single event that convinced me.

It was an overwhelming collection of small things.

The way she carried herself.

The way she treated other people.

Her character.

Her steadiness.

The way our values and priorities seemed to align naturally.

None of those things alone felt like a defining moment, but taken together they made the decision feel obvious.

Over time I've realized that strong marriages often begin this way. They are not built on drama or chaos. They are built on character, consistency, and shared direction.

One thing that has always stood out to me about my wife is her willingness to support our family through change. Early in our marriage she left her job and relocated to be with me. Since then she has done that several times as different opportunities or moves have come along.

Thankfully she is a registered nurse, which means employment has never been difficult to find in new places. Even so, I have never taken her flexibility for granted.

Relocating your career, rebuilding routines, and adjusting to new environments takes sacrifice.

What has always surprised me—in the best possible way—is how willing she has been to support changes that she believes will help our family. She has consistently shown a level of flexibility and commitment that I deeply respect.

Marriage has taught me many things over the years.

Some lessons came quickly. Others took time. And there are still many aspects of marriage that I know I have not experienced yet.

When I think about the household my wife and I are trying to build, it is centered around roles that we both understand and respect.

I see my responsibility as being the provider, the protector, the enforcer when necessary, and the steady hand when life becomes uncertain. Those responsibilities do not come from ego or authority. They come from a sense of duty. A husband should carry weight for his family.

My wife fills a role that is just as important. She is the nurturer, the organizer, and the loving presence that keeps the rhythm of our home moving forward. She brings warmth, care, and structure in ways that I could never replicate on my own.

Our roles are different, but they are deeply complementary.

Faith sits at the center of everything we try to build.

We eat together as a family several nights each week. We pray together. We go to church together. We talk openly about God and what it means to live according to the principles we believe in.

Those rhythms are intentional.

They do not happen by accident.

When big decisions arise, we do not rush into them. We pray about them—often many times. We talk through them carefully and wait until we both feel a strong sense of conviction before moving forward.

Whether it is a career change, a move, or another major decision for our family, we try to make sure we are pursuing something we believe God has guided us toward.

That does not mean every decision turns out perfectly. Life does not work that way. But it does mean we try to move forward with purpose, with prayer, and with the belief that our marriage and family are part of something bigger than ourselves.

Marriage is one of the most important commitments a person can make, yet it is often misunderstood.

It requires humility, sacrifice, patience, and a willingness to grow.

It exposes selfishness. It demands forgiveness. It forces two imperfect people to learn how to build something meaningful together over time.

When it is done well, however, it becomes one of the greatest sources of stability, joy, and strength a family can have.

I did not write this book because I believe I have marriage fully figured out.

I wrote it because I have been married long enough to have learned some things, to still be learning many things, and to know there are seasons of marriage that only time will reveal.

This book reflects that reality.

The first section explores what experience has already taught me about marriage.

The second section looks at lessons I am still learning as life and family continue to evolve.

The final section acknowledges what I do not yet know—because there are seasons of marriage I simply have not experienced yet.

I have not raised teenagers.

I have not navigated the empty nest.

I have not experienced what fifty years of marriage looks like.

Those seasons will come in time.

For now, these pages reflect what I have learned so far along the way.

Part I

What I've Learned

Chapter 1
Respect Is the Foundation

When I think about the difference between marriages that endure and marriages that fall apart, one word rises above everything else.

Respect.

Not chemistry.

Not attraction.

Not even communication.

Respect.

A lack of respect, in one form or another, is almost always present in marriages that fail. Sometimes it shows up loudly. Other times it creeps in slowly through small behaviors that seem harmless at first but gradually erode the relationship.

Respect is the foundation everything else in marriage is built on.

Without it, the structure cannot hold.

What Respect Meant to Me Early On

From the beginning, I understood that respect meant certain things inside a marriage.

It meant that disagreements were handled privately, but unity was presented publicly.

Every couple will disagree. That is part of living life together. But when those disagreements become public entertainment—when spouses criticize each other in front of friends, family, or coworkers—the damage goes deeper than people often realize.

Respect means protecting the relationship in front of others.

It also means placing your spouse above everyone else.

Marriage is a commitment that requires loyalty not just in words, but in daily decisions. Friends, coworkers, and even extended family can never outrank the person you chose to spend your life with.

Respect also means honoring the vows that were made.

Marriage is not just a romantic relationship. It is a covenant built on commitment. When two people stand together and make those promises, they are agreeing to something larger than their own feelings in any particular moment.

Respect means remembering that commitment, even when circumstances become difficult.

When Respect Disappears

Over the years, I have seen marriages where respect slowly disappeared.

Rarely does it happen overnight.

Often it shows up in subtle ways first.

Sometimes it appears in jokes that carry a little too much truth underneath them. A spouse makes a comment that gets a laugh from the room, but the humor has an edge to it.

Sometimes it shows up as public criticism. One spouse complains about what the other person does not do or fails to do. Instead of addressing concerns privately, the frustration becomes part of public conversation.

Comparison is another place where respect often begins to erode.

When someone starts comparing their spouse to other people—other husbands, other wives, other families—it creates a quiet resentment that can grow over time. Comparison is a thief of joy in many areas of life, but it is particularly destructive inside a marriage.

Another sign of fading respect is a lack of appreciation.

When someone no longer recognizes the effort their spouse is making, even when that effort is imperfect, the relationship begins to weaken. Marriage requires constant investment from both people. When that investment goes unnoticed or unappreciated, it becomes harder to sustain.

These things may seem small in isolation, but together they chip away at the respect that holds a marriage together.

Respect in Our Own Marriage

My wife and I are far from perfect, but there are certain boundaries we have always tried to maintain.

We do not yell at each other.

We do not cuss, fight, or feud in ways that create lasting damage.

That does not mean we never disagree. Of course we do. Every couple does. But we try to handle disagreements with a level of self-control and respect that protects the relationship.

Another boundary we have always tried to maintain is privacy.

Disagreements do not need audiences.

The details of our marriage are not meant to become stories for family gatherings or conversations with friends. What happens between us stays between us.

We also make a point not to portray each other negatively to other people.

Speaking poorly about your spouse may seem harmless in the moment, but those habits slowly reshape the way you see each other. Over time, the narrative becomes more negative, and respect begins to fade.

Protecting each other's reputation—even in small conversations—is one of the ways respect stays strong.

Respect and Leadership

Respect also plays an important role in leadership within the household.

In our home, I believe the husband should lead.

That leadership does not mean control or domination. It means responsibility. A husband sets the tone for the household.

He is responsible for the direction of the family, the atmosphere in the home, and the example being set for the children.

But leadership cannot exist without credibility.

If a man fails to lead well—if he avoids responsibility, behaves poorly, or fails to live up to the standards he expects from others—he will eventually lose the respect required to lead.

Respect cannot be demanded.

It must be earned and maintained through consistent character.

At the same time, leadership that is constantly undermined cannot function properly either. When respect disappears, the structure of the household begins to weaken.

Learning How My Wife Experiences Respect

One of the things marriage has taught me over time is that respect is not always experienced the same way by different people.

What feels respectful to one person might not carry the same meaning for someone else.

Over the years, I have learned a lot about how my wife views respect, and that understanding has helped me respect her in ways that resonate with her personally.

We are all wired differently. Some things that would not bother me very much might be deeply important to her. And there are things that might seem small to me that carry much more weight in her eyes.

There have been times when I have unintentionally let her down by not standing as firmly on something as she would have liked. It was not done out of disregard. It was simply a place where I did not fully understand how strongly she felt about the issue.

Time and experience have helped me recognize those moments better.

Marriage has a way of teaching you how your spouse sees the world. If you are paying attention, you begin to notice the places where respect matters most to them.

Learning those things—and adjusting accordingly—is one of the ways respect grows stronger over time.

When Respect Is Lost

When respect begins to erode in a marriage, the problem is urgent.

It is not something that should be ignored or allowed to drift.

Respect requires two things.

First, you have to be someone worthy of respect. Your actions, your decisions, and the way you carry yourself should reflect the kind of person your spouse can believe in.

Second, you must expect respect in return.

A healthy marriage cannot function if one person consistently tolerates disrespect. Boundaries matter. Standards matter. A marriage built on respect requires both people to protect that foundation.

Why Respect Matters So Much

Respect binds everything else together.

Love grows where respect exists.

Loyalty strengthens where respect exists.

Sacrifice becomes easier when respect exists.

Understanding deepens when respect exists.

But when respect disappears, those things slowly begin to fade as well.

You cannot build a lasting marriage on attraction alone.

You cannot build it on feelings alone.

You cannot build it on convenience.

A strong marriage is built on a deeper foundation.

It is built on mutual respect between two people committed to honoring each other and the life they are building together.

When respect thrives, a marriage can endure almost anything.

When it disappears, almost nothing can save it.

Chapter 2
Out-Serve Each Other

After respect, one of the habits that has strengthened our marriage the most is surprisingly simple.

We try to out-serve each other.

It's not a competition in the traditional sense. There's no scoreboard and no keeping track. It's simply a mindset that both people bring into the marriage: looking for ways to make the other person's life easier.

Serving your spouse does not require grand gestures.

Most of the time it shows up in small, ordinary moments.

Early in our marriage, my wife was always willing to serve. That attitude made an impression on me quickly. I've always tried to look out for other people as well, so it felt natural for both of us to operate that way.

When she worked late shifts or overnight as a nurse, I would try to let her sleep the next morning. If she had a long week, I'd try to lighten the load where I could.

On weekends, if I was the first one up, I'd try to have breakfast ready. If one of us had a rough night and had the chance to stay in bed a little longer, the other would try to make that happen.

These are not dramatic sacrifices.

But small acts of service add up over time.

They create a rhythm inside the marriage where both people feel supported.

Serving Instead of Competing

You can often see the difference between healthy marriages and struggling ones in this area.

Some couples seem to operate like teammates.

Others look like competitors.

I don't know that I would describe it as open competition, but you sometimes see marriages where people clearly are not on the same team. One person is focused primarily on their own needs, their own time, and their own priorities.

The attitude becomes, "I'm going to get mine, and everyone else can wait."

That mindset slowly turns a marriage into something one-sided.

When both people operate that way, resentment usually follows.

But when both people are looking for ways to serve each other, something different happens.

The relationship becomes cooperative rather than transactional.

Picking Each Other Up

Serving your spouse often shows up in simple ways.

When one person is worn down, the other steps in.

If my wife has had a long week, I might run an errand, throw in a load of laundry, or handle something around the house that normally would fall on her list.

If I've had a tough stretch, she does the same for me.

Sometimes service means sacrificing a little bit of personal time so the other person can have some.

Those adjustments may not seem significant in the moment, but over time they communicate something powerful: "We are in this together."

Don't Keep Score

One lesson that became clear to me very quickly came after our son was born.

Early on I remember thinking something like, "I've already changed three diapers today."

It was meant half jokingly, but it taught me something important almost immediately.

Keeping score in marriage never ends well.

Diapers are a perfect example. If you are around and they need changing, just do it. Counting how many you've done compared to the other person does nothing but create unnecessary tension.

Marriage works best when both people simply step in where they are needed.

When you stop tracking who has done more, service becomes natural again.

Growing in Service

Serving each other also requires humility.

It means recognizing that you may not always do it perfectly.

For example, I have never been very good at giving foot rubs.

When my wife and I first started dating, I was pretty terrible at it. I'm still not great today, but I've improved over time.

It might sound like a small thing, but even that is part of learning how to serve your spouse better.

Marriage teaches you where the other person feels cared for, and sometimes that requires stretching yourself beyond what feels natural.

Over time you begin to anticipate what your spouse needs.

You start noticing when they are overwhelmed, tired, or carrying too much responsibility.

And when you see it, you step in without needing to be asked.

A Supportive Partner

My wife has always been incredibly supportive, especially during busy or demanding seasons at work.

Now that she manages our home and homeschools our son, she will often ask me a simple question during the day:

"How can I help you today?"

The honest answer most of the time is that I'm okay. In fact, it sometimes feels uncomfortable trying to think of something she could do, because she already carries so much responsibility for our family.

But that question reflects the heart behind service.

It's the mindset of someone who is constantly looking for ways to support the other person.

And when both people bring that mindset into the marriage, the relationship becomes stronger.

The Result

When two people consistently look for ways to serve each other, something powerful happens.

The marriage becomes less about keeping score and more about carrying the load together.

Respect creates the foundation.

Service strengthens the structure.

And over time, those small acts of care become the beams that hold the marriage together.

Not because life is always easy.

But because neither person is carrying it alone.

Chapter 3
Just Say It

One of the simplest lessons I have learned in marriage is also one of the easiest to ignore.

Sometimes you just have to say it.

Problems rarely improve when they remain unspoken. In fact, most of the time they quietly grow larger the longer they sit unresolved.

I have learned this lesson the hard way more than once.

When I get frustrated, my natural reaction is often to get quiet. Instead of saying what is bothering me, I sometimes keep it to myself and try to move past it.

The problem with that approach is that the issue does not actually disappear.

It just stays there longer than it should.

Many times the frustration could have been resolved quickly if I had simply said something early on.

Speaking Up Early

There have also been moments when I chose to speak up right away, and the difference was noticeable.

Sometimes it is as simple as saying something like, *"That wasn't cool,"* or *"Where are we going with this?"*

Those types of responses are not meant to start an argument. They are simply a way of expressing that something does not sit right.

When things are addressed early, they often lose their power to grow into something bigger.

The tension gets acknowledged, talked through, and resolved before it turns into a much larger issue.

Why People Avoid Saying Things

Most people do not avoid difficult conversations because they enjoy conflict.

In fact, many people avoid them because they dislike conflict.

I do not fear conflict, but I do not prefer it either. I think that is a fairly normal place to land.

Some people fear confrontation entirely.

Others seem to thrive in it.

But many people simply stay quiet because they do not want to hurt someone's feelings.

The challenge with staying quiet is that frustration does not usually disappear.

Instead, it builds.

And when frustration builds long enough, it often comes out all at once.

When that happens, the issue becomes much larger than it would have been if it had simply been addressed early.

Learning From the Hard Moments

My wife and I have not always handled disagreements perfectly.

We have yelled before.

We have said things we should not have said.

There have been one or two arguments that were bigger than they should have been.

But those moments taught us something important.

Fighting your spouse in that way leaves a mark.

After a real battle with your spouse, it tends to stick with you. The words, the tone, and the emotions linger longer than either person wants them to.

Experiencing that a couple of times was enough to make us realize that going down that road does not help either of us.

Now when disagreements happen, we try to handle them differently.

We still disagree sometimes.

We might occasionally bicker back and forth.

And there are still moments when I get frustrated and go quiet, even though I know that is not always the best response.

But we try to keep one important perspective in mind.

We are on the same team.

We have the same goals.

And the problem is never supposed to become more important than the relationship.

Talking It Through

One of the most helpful things we have done after some of those bigger disagreements is simply sit down and talk.

Not to argue again.

Just to understand.

We have asked questions like:

How did we get there?

Why did we let something small turn into something bigger?

Could we have handled it differently?

Was it even as big of a deal as it felt in the moment?

And what do we do if the same situation comes up again?

Those conversations matter.

Working through those questions together has often left us in a better place than we were before the disagreement ever started.

Instead of letting frustration sit unresolved, the conversation helps both of us understand each other better.

And that understanding strengthens the relationship moving forward.

Being Willing to Be Wrong

Another part of communication in marriage is being willing to admit when you are wrong.

That happens more often than most people probably expect.

Sometimes I realize I am wrong while we are talking through something.

Other times I realize it later, after thinking about the situation more carefully.

And occasionally, after talking things through honestly, we simply agree to disagree and move forward.

Not every difference has to become a long debate.

Depending on the situation, sometimes the healthiest thing to do is acknowledge the disagreement and move on.

The Value of Saying It

Marriage works best when communication stays honest and direct.

That does not mean every thought needs to be spoken immediately or without consideration.

But it does mean that important things should not remain buried.

When something matters, it needs to be said.

Not aggressively.

Not carelessly.

Just honestly.

Because more often than not, problems that feel complicated become surprisingly simple once they are brought into the open.

Chapter 4

Sacrifice Is Required

Marriage requires a level of selflessness that is easy to underestimate.

Most people understand the idea in theory. When you stand at the altar, you know that marriage involves commitment, compromise, and putting someone else ahead of yourself.

But the reality of sacrifice becomes clearer once life begins unfolding.

Over time, marriage asks both people to adjust their plans, their priorities, and sometimes even their entire direction in life.

And when both people are willing to do that for each other, the relationship becomes stronger.

The Willingness to Move

One of the clearest examples of sacrifice in our marriage has been the number of moves we have made for my career.

Since 2016, we have lived in four different towns across three different states. During that same time I have taken on six different roles.

It has been a lot of change in a relatively short period of time.

Anyone who has moved even once knows how disruptive it can be. You leave familiar routines, relationships, and places that have become comfortable.

In some marriages, the conversation that begins with *"It might be time to move"* can quickly turn into a major point of conflict.

In extreme cases, it can even end the relationship.

I have been incredibly fortunate that my wife has approached those conversations differently.

She has always been willing to go.

More than that, she has embraced the challenge that comes with it.

But that does not mean the moves were easy.

At one point we were living in southwest Georgia and had built a life we truly loved there.

We loved our home. We loved our church. I enjoyed my job, and we were close to family.

It was comfortable.

It was familiar.

It was a life we loved.

But after about five years in that role, I had begun to feel a little stale professionally. I needed a new challenge, and eventually an opportunity came along that required us to move.

Accepting that opportunity meant packing up a life we truly loved.

I still remember the day we left that house.

There were tears as we pulled out of the driveway for the last time.

We had gotten married in the backyard of that house. We had brought our son home from the hospital to that house.

So many meaningful moments had happened there.

Leaving was incredibly hard.

But my wife never hesitated. She supported the decision fully, even though it meant leaving a place that meant a lot to both of us.

Looking back, it is clear that my career would not be where it is today if she had not been willing to make that sacrifice alongside me.

Supporting Each Other's Interests

Sacrifice in marriage does not only show up in big life decisions like moving.

Often it appears in the smaller ways spouses support each other's interests and passions.

My wife has always been incredibly supportive of the things I enjoy.

I love to deer hunt, and she fully supports that hobby whenever possible.

I am also a big Florida Gators fan. Watching them play football, basketball, baseball, and other sports is something I genuinely enjoy.

Instead of seeing that as something separate from our life together, she has leaned into it and joined in. Her willingness to support and participate in things that matter to me has meant a lot.

Those moments may seem small on the surface, but they reflect something deeper.

They show a willingness to prioritize the happiness of the other person.

When Sacrifice Becomes One-Sided

Of course, sacrifice becomes much harder when it starts to feel like a one-way street.

That is true in marriage and in almost every other type of relationship.

If one person is constantly sacrificing while the other person rarely does, frustration and resentment are likely to grow.

Sometimes that imbalance happens because expectations are not communicated clearly.

Other times the request itself may not be presented well.

An idea that should have been discussed together may come across as a demand. What might have been intended as a conversation can feel more like an ultimatum if it is not communicated thoughtfully.

Sometimes it takes patience and careful conversation to explain why something matters and to help the other person understand the bigger picture.

In many cases, a little internal "selling" may be required.

But when both people are willing to listen and consider each other's perspective, those conversations can lead to decisions that strengthen the relationship instead of dividing it.

Choosing the Team Over the Individual

At its core, sacrifice in marriage reflects a simple truth.

You are no longer operating as an individual.

You are part of a team.

When you sacrifice for your spouse or your family, you are choosing the success of the team over the preferences of the individual.

That mindset is common in team sports. Players accept that their role may change depending on what helps the team succeed.

The same principle applies to marriage.

Sometimes one person carries more of the load for a season.

Other times the roles reverse.

But when both people are committed to the same outcome, those sacrifices begin to feel less like losses and more like investments.

The Strength That Sacrifice Builds

Sacrifice does not weaken a healthy marriage.

It strengthens it.

When a spouse gives something up for the benefit of the relationship, it communicates something powerful.

It shows that the marriage itself matters more than personal convenience.

It shows that the relationship is bigger than individual preferences.

And it reminds both people that they are building something together.

Over time, those sacrifices become part of the shared story of the marriage.

They are the moments that prove the relationship is built on something deeper than comfort.

They show that two people are willing to give in order to be part of something greater than themselves.

Chapter 5
Protect the Marriage

A strong marriage does not maintain itself automatically.

Even healthy relationships require protection.

Life is full of outside pressures, opinions, distractions, and influences that can slowly weaken a marriage if couples are not intentional about guarding the relationship.

Protecting your marriage means recognizing that what you and your spouse are building together is valuable enough to defend.

Sometimes that protection shows up in big decisions.

More often, it appears in small habits and boundaries that keep the relationship healthy over time.

Disagreements Don't Need an Audience

One of the simplest ways to protect a marriage is to be mindful about where disagreements happen.

If you spend enough time around other people, it is almost inevitable that you will eventually disagree with your spouse in front of someone else.

It happens.

But those moments should be the exception, not the norm.

Disagreements do not need audiences.

When a conflict begins to unfold in front of other people, it introduces unnecessary complications. Sometimes the people watching may unintentionally insert themselves into the situation. Other times someone in the room may not have the best intentions toward you or your spouse.

In some cases, people may even be waiting for moments like that to appear.

Allowing conflict to play out publicly creates opportunities for outside voices to influence something that should remain between two people.

Most disagreements are better handled privately.

When couples learn to step away and address issues on their own, they remove many of the outside pressures that can make conflict worse.

Speaking Well of Your Spouse

Another way to protect your marriage is by being careful about how you talk about your spouse to other people.

Speaking negatively about your spouse might seem harmless in the moment. Sometimes people do it jokingly. Other times it comes out during frustration.

But over time, those habits can create damage.

It is not a good look to criticize your spouse to other people.

It is an even worse position to agree when someone else starts doing it.

When someone begins complaining about their spouse, it can be tempting to join in or offer your own frustrations. But conversations like that rarely lead anywhere productive.

Eventually that couple may work things out and move forward, and the people who participated in tearing down the relationship are left in an uncomfortable spot.

In most cases, it is simply better not to offer an opinion.

Protecting your spouse's reputation—even in casual conversations—is one of the ways you protect the marriage itself.

Guarding Your Privacy

My wife and I have also tried to be intentional about keeping the details of our marriage private.

That does not mean we live in isolation or never seek advice when it is needed.

But we try to minimize spreading our business around unnecessarily.

Every couple faces challenges. Those challenges do not need to become public conversations.

When personal issues remain between the people who are actually responsible for solving them, the relationship stays healthier.

Privacy creates space for honesty and trust to grow.

Protecting Time Together

Another important way to guard a marriage is by protecting time together.

Life has a way of becoming incredibly busy.

Work responsibilities grow. Parenting requires energy. Daily responsibilities pile up.

Over time it becomes easy to drift into routines where the marriage itself receives less attention.

My wife and I try to be mindful of that.

Dating your spouse may not always look the same once you have kids, but you can still be intentional about creating time together.

Sometimes it is as simple as having a night where we binge-watch a show we have both been wanting to see.

Other nights we cook at home and sit together for a while just catching up.

Those moments may seem small, but they matter.

They create space to reconnect and stay in rhythm with each other.

The Danger of Drift

One of the biggest threats to a marriage is not conflict.

It is drift.

When a couple has been together for many years, it is easy to assume the relationship will simply take care of itself.

But marriage, like anything valuable, requires maintenance.

Life moves quickly, and sometimes couples lose momentum without realizing it.

Work becomes demanding. Children require attention. Responsibilities multiply.

Before long, the relationship that once felt like the center of life can slowly slide down the priority list.

The obvious drifts are easy to notice.

It is the small ones you have to stay on guard against.

Simple Habits That Protect a Marriage

Fortunately, protecting a marriage does not require complicated strategies.

Often it comes down to simple habits practiced consistently.

Keep dating your spouse.

Communicate openly.

Avoid creating unnecessary conflict or inviting others into your disagreements.

Pray for each other.

Talk about the things that matter most—your hopes, your goals, your dreams, and the direction you want your family to go.

These habits may seem ordinary, but over time they create a powerful sense of unity.

Guard What You've Built

Marriage is one of the most important relationships a person will ever have.

Like anything valuable, it deserves to be protected.

That protection does not require perfection.

It simply requires awareness.

When couples are intentional about guarding their relationship—protecting their privacy, their time together, and their respect for each other—they create an environment where the marriage can continue to grow stronger over time.

Because what you are building together is worth protecting.

Chapter 6
Be Intentional

Strong marriages do not happen by accident.

They are built through daily choices.

Being intentional in marriage means consistently choosing your spouse—over people, places, things, everything.

It means moving with purpose.

It means making decisions with long-term goals in mind rather than simply reacting to whatever the day brings.

When a couple is intentional about their relationship, they are actively building something together.

Without that intentionality, it becomes easy for the relationship to slowly drift.

Choosing Your Spouse Every Day

Intentional marriage begins with a simple idea: consistently choosing your partner.

Marriage is not just a commitment made once at the altar. It is a commitment that gets renewed through everyday decisions.

Those decisions often appear small in the moment.

Choosing to listen instead of dismiss.

Choosing to support instead of criticize.

Choosing to consider what is best for the relationship rather than what is easiest for yourself.

Over time, those small choices shape the direction of the marriage.

When both spouses are intentional about choosing each other, the relationship grows stronger.

The Danger of Busy Seasons

One of the seasons where intentionality matters most is when life becomes busy.

Work demands increase.

Children require more attention.

Schedules fill up.

Responsibilities multiply.

Those seasons can quietly create distance if couples are not careful.

When someone begins to feel unnoticed or unappreciated for too long, the marriage enters dangerous territory.

If there isn't enough equity in the relationship bank, those feelings can quickly grow into resentment.

That is why intentionality matters so much during busy seasons.

It reminds both people that the relationship still deserves attention and care.

Making Decisions Together

Intentional marriages also approach important decisions carefully.

My wife and I try to talk through the decisions we face.

We pray about them.

We think through the options and eventually draw our own conclusions.

Then we share those thoughts with each other and decide how to move forward.

We have practiced that process many times.

When work opportunities have come up.

When we have searched for homes.

When we have talked about expanding our family.

Even during difficult seasons—such as when we experienced miscarriages.

And now as she carries our unborn son.

Each of those moments required thoughtful conversations and prayer before moving forward.

Intentional decisions require patience.

But those conversations help ensure that both people feel heard and valued as the family moves forward together.

Leadership and Trust

In our marriage, my wife trusts me to make many of the decisions that shape our family's direction.

She allows me to lead in that way and supports where I land.

Even when I sometimes ask her to carry more of the decision-making, she often defers back to me.

That trust is something I take seriously.

Because of that, I try to make sure I am always considering her perspective and honoring her role in the relationship.

While I may bring forward many ideas, I never pursue something important unless she is on board with it.

Intentional leadership means making decisions that serve the whole family—not just the person making them.

When Intentionality Disappears

When couples stop being intentional, the effects are rarely immediate.

They appear slowly.

Service fades.

Consideration fades.

Putting the other person first becomes less frequent.

Distance begins to grow.

And that distance allows the outside world to slowly gain a foothold inside the relationship.

The foundation weakens.

Cracks begin to show.

I cannot say that I have personally witnessed many marriages fall apart from the inside.

But once cracks start to appear, it often becomes obvious what has been missing.

Intentionality is one of the things that prevents that process from taking hold.

Building Together

Marriage works best when both people remember they are building something together.

My wife and I try to maintain habits that reinforce that mindset.

We eat together as a family multiple times each week.

We talk about the direction of our family.

We share ideas, plans, and goals for the future.

I may bring forward many of the ideas, but the direction we take is always something we agree on together.

Those conversations help keep us aligned.

And alignment is one of the most powerful ways to strengthen a marriage over time.

Move With Purpose

Intentional marriages do not drift.

They move with purpose.

They make decisions thoughtfully.

They prioritize the relationship even when life becomes busy.

And they consistently choose the good of the partnership over the convenience of the moment.

Because the strongest marriages are not built by accident.

They are built on purpose.

Chapter 7
Your Marriage Sets the Tone for the Family

The relationship between a husband and wife does more than shape the marriage itself.

It shapes the entire household.

Children watch everything. They notice how their parents speak to each other, how they handle disagreements, and how they show love and respect.

Whether parents realize it or not, the marriage relationship becomes the tone setter for the entire family.

It establishes the atmosphere of the home and the example that children grow up watching every day.

The Foundation of the Home

I believe it is biblical that one man and one woman should join together in marriage.

That union becomes the foundation of the family.

When that foundation is healthy and strong, it creates stability for everything built on top of it.

Within that structure there is a balance.

One voice that helps set the tone and direction.

Another that nurtures and strengthens the home.

Discipline and guidance working alongside care and encouragement.

Both roles are important.

Children benefit from hearing both voices and learning from both perspectives.

A healthy family environment requires that balance.

What Children See

Children do not just hear what their parents say.

They see how their parents live.

My wife and I want our son to see certain things in our home.

We want him to see us love each other.

We want him to see us pray openly.

We want him to see us apologize when we are wrong.

We want him to see us treat each other with respect and consideration.

And we want him to see that we are united.

Those examples teach lessons that words alone cannot communicate.

Children learn more from what they observe than what they are told.

Leadership in the Home

Leadership inside the home means setting the tone, the pace, and the direction for the family.

It means rising to the occasion when responsibility calls.

Sometimes that leadership looks like providing for the family.

Other times it means nurturing, guiding, disciplining, or simply being present when something is needed.

Leadership in the home is not about control.

It is about responsibility.

It is about recognizing that the example being set today will influence the people your children become tomorrow.

Faith at the Center

Faith plays a central role in our home.

Our son knows the Lord.

He knows the place that faith holds in our lives.

He sees our commitment to it.

He understands that our standards and expectations come from something greater than ourselves.

Faith is not just something we talk about.

It shapes the way we live.

It influences the way we make decisions, the way we treat each other, and the way we approach life as a family.

Even at a young age, our son already shows how much he is absorbing.

He will reference Bible stories or talk about people from Scripture that he has learned about.

He enjoys roughhousing and pretending to have "battles," and one of his favorites is pretending that I am Goliath and he is David.

Moments like that remind me how closely children are watching and learning from the environment around them.

When faith sits at the center of the household, it provides direction that goes beyond individual opinions or preferences.

It becomes the compass that guides how the family lives.

The Environment a Marriage Creates

When a marriage is healthy, the environment inside the home reflects that health.

There is unity.

There is consistency.

Children know what their parents stand for and what they expect.

The home becomes a place where love and structure exist together.

But when the marriage struggles, children often feel that tension as well.

The tone of the marriage eventually becomes the tone of the household.

That is why investing in the marriage relationship is not only important for the couple—it is important for the entire family.

Because the way a husband and wife treat each other will eventually become the culture of the home.

A Season of Continued Learning

Marriage has already taught me a great deal.

The principles in the previous chapters are things I believe strongly because I have seen them work in my own home and in the homes of others. Respect, service, communication, sacrifice, protection, and intentionality have proven to be essential foundations for a healthy marriage.

But marriage is not something you figure out once and then move on from.

It continues to grow and change over time.

Every new season of life introduces new challenges and new lessons. Careers change. Families grow. Responsibilities increase. Experiences—both joyful and painful—shape the relationship in ways you could not have predicted when you first said your vows.

Some of the things I once thought I fully understood about marriage have become more complex as time has passed. Other lessons have become clearer through experience.

In many ways, marriage is a lifelong process of learning.

The next section reflects that reality.

These chapters are not about lessons I feel certain I have mastered. They are reflections on things I am still learning as our marriage continues to grow and evolve.

Because the truth is that no matter how many years pass, marriage still has more to teach.

Part II

What I'm Learning

Chapter 8
Marriage Evolves Over Time

One of the things I am learning about marriage is that it never stays the same.

The relationship you begin with is not the same relationship you grow into.

Life changes. Responsibilities increase. Seasons shift. And as those changes happen, the marriage changes with them.

If couples expect marriage to stay exactly the way it was in the beginning, they will eventually be disappointed. The goal is not to preserve the early version of the relationship forever.

The goal is to grow with each other as life evolves.

Early Years and Where We Are Now

When my wife and I first got together, life looked very different than it does today.

We were younger. Our weekends were often more spontaneous. Life had fewer responsibilities and fewer long-term plans.

Now we have a child, with another on the way.

We have matured.

Our weekends are often calmer. Some of our greatest joys now come from simple things—spending time at home, visiting family, or being around friends.

Those changes do not mean the relationship has lost something.

In many ways, it has simply grown into something deeper.

Seasons That Shape a Marriage

Certain seasons of life leave a lasting mark on a marriage.

For us, moving has been one of those seasons.

Each move brings its own upheaval. There is the stress of relocating, settling into a new community, and rebuilding routines.

We joke that it often takes a year or more before we finally get a house arranged the way we want it.

But eventually each place begins to feel like home.

Our losses have also shaped our story.

They do not define us, but they are part of our journey.

Those experiences make our son Will—and Jack when he arrives—even greater blessings.

Seasons like that deepen a marriage.

They remind you what truly matters.

Growing Goals

When we first started out, it was just the two of us.

We were focused on the present and did not spend much time thinking about life decades down the road.

Now we are twelve years into our relationship and seven years into our marriage.

The conversations look different.

We talk about our future more intentionally.

We talk about business ideas, financial goals, and the possibility of retiring early and eventually living near the beach.

Marriage has a way of shifting your perspective over time.

What once felt far away begins to feel closer, and planning together becomes more important.

Love Is Not Enough

One thing I have come to understand more clearly over time is that love by itself is not enough to sustain a long-term relationship.

Love is important.

But it must be supported by other things.

Communication.

Respect.

Alignment.

A willingness to address issues before they grow into larger problems.

Without those things, even relationships that begin with strong feelings can struggle over time.

Growing Together

Some couples grow together through life's changes.

Others slowly grow apart.

I believe the difference often comes down to alignment and communication.

When couples stop talking honestly with each other, small differences can quietly widen into larger gaps.

Respect can erode.

Drift can take hold.

But when couples remain aligned—when they continue communicating, respecting each other, and addressing issues early—they are far more likely to grow together through each new season.

The Same People and Different People

Another thing I am learning is that in some ways my wife and I are still the same people we were when we first got together.

But in other ways, we are completely different.

Life has changed us.

Experiences have shaped us.

Responsibilities have stretched us.

Watching my wife become a mother, a homemaker, and a homeschool teacher has been incredible.

Those roles have revealed strengths and qualities that were not visible in the early years of our relationship.

As life evolves, I am learning that marriage requires adjusting your approach along the way.

The goal is not simply to hold onto what worked in the beginning.

It is to keep adapting as life changes and continue building the future together.

Chapter 9
People Experience Love and Respect Differently

One of the things I am still learning about marriage is that people often experience love and respect in different ways.

Two people may want the same things in a relationship, but they may experience those things very differently.

Sometimes it takes honest conversations to recognize what has been missing.

When It Was Pointed Out

I first began to understand this when my wife told me directly.

For a long time I thought the idea of "love languages" was a little overplayed. I was skeptical of the concept and didn't put much weight behind it.

Over time, though, I've become less skeptical.

I tend to express love through giving.

That might look like gifts, helping with things, or acts of service.

My wife tends to express love through affection and touch.

That has never come as naturally to me.

It's an area of our marriage where I know I still need to improve.

Learning that difference helped me realize that even when I believed I was showing love, it might not always be received the way I expected.

When Perspectives Don't Line Up

Another way those differences show up is in how we process interactions with other people.

There are times when I think an exchange with someone else is unnecessary or not worth spending much time thinking about—especially if it involves some kind of disagreement.

My natural instinct is to avoid situations that create unnecessary conflict.

Avoiding conflict doesn't mean I'm afraid of it. I just don't see the need to engage in situations that don't seem productive.

My wife approaches those situations differently.

If she has an interaction that leaves her uncertain—especially if there was tension or disagreement—she often wants to talk it through.

She'll bounce the interaction off of me to see whether she handled it correctly or whether she might have been wrong.

Sometimes those are moments where we don't mesh perfectly.

If I believe the situation wasn't important to begin with, my instinct can be to dismiss it.

But for her, those conversations provide closure.

Learning to recognize that difference has helped me become more patient and more willing to engage in those conversations when they matter to her.

Respect From Different Angles

In many ways, my wife and I share very similar views on respect.

The differences usually appear in smaller moments.

Sometimes the things that matter deeply to her may not immediately stand out to me as important.

The lesson I'm continuing to learn is that those things still deserve attention.

Respect in marriage isn't only about the big principles.

It also means making sure the things that matter to your spouse are not casually dismissed.

The Danger of Assumptions

One of the easiest mistakes to make in marriage is assuming that your spouse should experience things the same way you do.

If something wouldn't bother you, it's easy to assume it shouldn't bother them either.

But people are not all wired the same way.

Expecting two different people to react to situations exactly the same way is unrealistic.

I know I've been guilty of that mindset before.

And when that assumption creeps in, it can create unnecessary frustration.

Understanding that people experience things differently helps create patience and empathy inside the relationship.

Learning the Changes

Another lesson I'm still learning is that people continue to evolve.

The person you marry will not stay exactly the same over time.

Life experiences change people.

Responsibilities change them.

New seasons of life reveal different priorities and perspectives.

Part of growing in marriage is learning to recognize those changes.

It means paying attention to how your spouse is evolving and being willing to explain the changes you are experiencing as well.

When both people are open about those shifts, it helps maintain alignment as the relationship grows.

Marriage works best when two people never stop learning each other.

Chapter 10
Balancing Work, Marriage, and Family

Providing for your family is a responsibility I take seriously.

It's my job, and it's something I'm proud to do.

Being able to provide for my family and allow my wife to stay home and teach our son is something I'm deeply grateful for. It means our son is raised in the environment we believe is best for him.

We aren't turning him over to strangers without knowing what influences are shaping his life.

We have a clear line of sight into what he's learning and what's being poured into his life.

That's something that matters a great deal to us.

Learning Balance

There was a season in my career when my balance wasn't very good.

Like many people early in their careers, I worked constantly. I didn't have many boundaries, and work could easily spill over into time that should have belonged to my family.

Eventually something became very clear to me.

If I died tomorrow, my job would be posted and someone else would replace me almost immediately.

That's just the reality of how the workplace functions.

But that isn't how it works at home.

A husband and father can't be replaced.

Once I fully understood that difference, I began to approach work differently.

I still give my best at work. I start early and work hard so the job gets done.

But when the workday ends, I shift into my role as a husband and father.

Those roles deserve my full attention too.

Understanding the Trade-Offs

One of the mistakes I see people make is constantly chasing more money or the next promotion in the name of providing for their family.

The intention may be good.

But sometimes the cost isn't fully understood.

People can miss critical moments in their children's lives while chasing the next raise, the next performance review, or the next promotion.

The extra income may help in certain ways.

But those opportunities can never replace time with your children when they are young.

Promotions eventually come and go.

But the years when your kids are small never come back.

Your promotion won't matter to your child when they're growing up.

What they will remember is whether you were present.

Whether you showed up.

Whether you were part of the moments that shaped their childhood.

My children will never have to wonder if their father was present.

And if that decision slows my professional growth, that's a trade I'm happy to make.

My Wife's Sacrifice

Another thing that keeps me motivated is the sacrifice my wife has made for our family.

She has multiple degrees and was very accomplished in her field.

But she stepped away from that career to focus on our home and our children.

That kind of sacrifice deserves respect.

It deserves effort.

Seeing her make that choice motivates me to work hard and perform well in my role as a provider.

If she is willing to make that kind of commitment for our family, the least I can do is give my best in the role I've been given.

Being Present

One of the things I'm still learning is how to be fully present with my family when I am home.

Setting boundaries with work is important.

But boundaries don't mean much if the time you create isn't used well.

It's easy to be physically present while still mentally distracted.

That's something I continue working on.

When I'm with my family, I want my attention to actually be there.

Marriage and parenting deserve more than leftover time and leftover energy.

They deserve presence.

Balancing work, marriage, and family will probably always require adjustment.

But one thing is clear to me.

Providing for your family matters.

Being present with them matters even more than that.

Chapter 11
Gratitude Strengthens a Marriage

One of the things I continue to learn in marriage is how important gratitude really is.

It's easy to notice the things that frustrate us.

It takes more effort to notice the things our spouse does well every day.

Gratitude keeps those things from going unseen.

And when gratitude disappears from a marriage, resentment can quietly take its place.

What I'm Grateful For

There are many things about my wife that I'm grateful for.

Her loyalty.

Her heart.

Her willingness to support and follow my leadership within our family.

The way she keeps our home running.

The sacrifices she has made for our family.

Those things are not small.

They require effort, discipline, and a constant willingness to put the needs of the family ahead of personal comfort.

Watching her carry those responsibilities has given me a deeper appreciation for everything she does.

The Danger of Going Unnoticed

I believe many marriages struggle when effort goes unnoticed for too long.

If someone consistently puts effort into their role in the relationship but never feels recognized for it, frustration can begin to grow.

People don't expect statues built in their honor for doing what they're supposed to do.

But they do want to know their effort is noticed.

When appreciation disappears, people can begin to feel taken for granted.

That's when resentment often starts to creep in.

The Everyday Things That Matter

Many of the things that deserve appreciation in a marriage are the everyday responsibilities that quietly keep life moving forward.

My wife works hard to make sure our home stays organized and functional.

She makes sure we eat—or at least have the opportunity to eat—three home-cooked meals most days.

She organizes our schedule and keeps us on track.

She makes sure the house stays clean and that our household runs the way it should.

Those responsibilities may not always draw attention, but they require constant effort.

Without someone managing those things, the home quickly falls into disorder.

Showing Gratitude

Gratitude shouldn't stay unspoken.

I try to acknowledge what my wife does and make sure she knows I see the effort she puts into our family.

Sometimes that means giving her time to decompress.

Sometimes it means making sure we still prioritize time together, like going on solo dates when we can.

And sometimes it means simply making sure our family has what we need—and as many of the things we want as possible.

Those are some of the ways I try to show appreciation for everything she does.

Learning to Say It

One thing I'm still learning is that the way I express love isn't always the way my wife experiences it most clearly.

My instinct is to show love through actions and gifts.

I naturally gravitate toward doing things or providing things.

But I'm learning that words can carry just as much weight—sometimes even more.

Taking the time to say what you appreciate about your spouse can mean a great deal.

Gratitude spoken out loud reinforces the value of the effort being made.

And in a marriage, that kind of recognition strengthens the relationship.

Looking Ahead

Marriage has already taught me many lessons.

Some of those lessons come from years of experience. Others come from mistakes, conversations, and moments that forced me to reflect on what really matters.

But there are still seasons of marriage I haven't experienced yet.

Our family is still young.

Our children are still small.

Many of the chapters of life that shape a long marriage are still ahead of us.

I haven't navigated the teenage years with my children yet.

I haven't experienced what life looks like when the house grows quiet after children move out.

And I haven't yet seen what marriage looks like after decades of growing old together.

Those seasons will bring their own challenges and their own lessons.

For now, all I can do is observe the marriages of people who are further down the road and think about the kind of husband I hope to be when those seasons arrive.

The following chapters aren't written from experience.

They are written from observation, reflection, and hope.

Because if marriage continues to teach me anything, it's that there is always more to learn.

Part III

What I Don't Know Yet

Chapter 12
Marriage Through the Teenage Years

One season of marriage I haven't experienced yet is raising teenagers.

Our son is still young, and another child is on the way, so I can't speak from personal experience about what that phase of life will look like inside our home.

But from observing other families, it's clear that the teenage years bring their own set of challenges.

Those challenges don't just affect the children.

They can affect the marriage too.

The Risk of Division

From what I've seen, teenagers can sometimes create division within a household—sometimes intentionally, and sometimes unintentionally.

Parents may disagree on how to handle certain situations.

One parent may lean toward discipline while the other leans toward patience.

One may want to give more freedom while the other prefers tighter boundaries.

Those differences can create tension if the parents aren't aligned.

Because of that, unity between husband and wife seems more important than ever during those years.

If the parents aren't on the same page, the household can quickly become divided.

The Balance of Space and Guidance

Another challenge I imagine parents face is balancing independence with oversight.

Teenagers naturally want more space.

They want the freedom to make more of their own decisions and explore the world around them.

But that freedom can also create concern.

Driving, distance from home, decision-making, outside influences, and relationships all begin to play a bigger role in their lives.

Parents must learn how to give their children room to grow while still providing the guidance and boundaries that keep them safe.

From the outside looking in, that balance seems difficult to manage.

Staying United

If there's one thing that seems especially important during those years, it's communication between husband and wife.

Decisions involving teenagers can carry long-term consequences.

Because of that, parents need to talk openly with each other and remain aligned.

That doesn't mean every decision will be easy.

But it likely means that unity matters more than winning an argument.

The goal shouldn't be getting your way.

The goal should be finding the best outcome for your child and your family.

That kind of unity requires trust and communication.

And when that trust is honored, it strengthens both the marriage and the family.

Learning From Others

I've seen parents navigate the teenage years well.

And when I see that, I have a great deal of respect for them.

Because I know it wasn't easy.

If anything, it seems like raising teenagers is becoming more difficult as the world continues to change.

The influences surrounding young people today are stronger and more constant than they were in previous generations.

That makes the role of parents—and the unity of a marriage—even more important.

Looking Ahead

When our children reach those years, my hope is that my wife and I will face them as a team.

We may not always get every decision right.

But if we stay aligned, communicate well, and focus on the best outcome for our family, we'll have a better chance of navigating that season successfully.

For now, the teenage years remain a chapter of marriage I'm still looking toward.

But from what I can see, it will be a season that requires patience, communication, and a strong partnership between husband and wife.

Chapter 13
The Empty Nest

Another season of marriage I haven't experienced yet is the empty nest.

After years of raising children, guiding them, and building life around their needs, there eventually comes a point when they leave home and begin building lives of their own.

When that happens, the house grows quiet again.

The marriage returns to what it once was at the very beginning—just two people.

From what I've observed, couples seem to handle that transition very differently.

Some appear happier and more connected than ever.

Others seem a little lost.

When the House Gets Quiet

My hypothesis—based purely on observation—is that couples who prioritized their relationship while raising children tend to handle the empty nest more smoothly.

Those who dated each other, stayed intentional, and continued investing in the marriage seem better prepared for that transition.

Couples who built their entire identity around parenting sometimes appear to struggle more once that role changes.

If the marriage relationship disappears during those years, couples may find themselves trying to rebuild it from scratch once the children are gone.

That doesn't mean the transition is easy for anyone.

But it may be easier for couples who stayed connected along the way.

Staying Connected While Raising Children

The idea that couples should remain connected while raising children has shown up several times throughout this book.

The more I observe families, the more convinced I am that this matters.

Parenting requires an incredible amount of attention, time, and energy.

It can easily consume nearly every moment of a couple's life for years.

Couples who continue dating, communicating, and prioritizing each other seem to enter the empty nest with a stronger foundation already in place.

What I Hope That Season Looks Like

When my wife and I eventually reach that stage of life, my hope is that the transition feels natural rather than disorienting.

I hope we stay connected during the years when our children are growing up so that the shift to an empty house feels like the start of a new chapter rather than the loss of the previous one.

Maybe some spontaneity returns.

Maybe there's more time for travel, fun, and simply enjoying each other's company again.

But more than anything, I hope we have been the kind of parents our children want to stay connected with.

I hope they want to visit.

I hope they want to vacation together.

I hope they want to remain close as adults.

If that happens, the empty nest won't feel empty at all.

It will simply be another season of life.

Learning From Couples Who Do It Well

I've seen couples navigate the empty nest in a healthy way.

One thing that stands out about those marriages is that they seem to genuinely enjoy each other's company.

They still have fun together.

They still laugh together.

Their relationship with God also seems to provide stability during that transition.

Faith gives their marriage a foundation that remains steady even when life changes.

When children move out, their purpose and connection remain.

They stay rooted in something deeper.

A Short Season in the Big Picture

One realization that stands out to me is how quickly the parenting years actually pass.

In most cases, parents may have somewhere between eighteen and twenty-two summers with their children living at home.

When you step back and look at it that way, it's a surprisingly short window of time.

It's both beautiful and a little sad to think about.

But it also serves as a reminder to be present during those years while they're happening.

Because before long, the house will grow quiet again.

And the marriage will enter a new chapter.

Chapter 14

Growing Old Together

One of the things I admire most is seeing couples who have been married for forty or fifty years.

When I see marriages that have lasted that long, there's a sense of respect that comes with it.

It's hard not to admire that kind of commitment.

There's something incredibly commendable about two people refusing to give up on each other.

Refusing to tap out.

Refusing to throw in the towel.

That level of dedication is impressive.

Marriages that endure for decades often seem defined by toughness, loyalty, trust, and commitment.

Those qualities don't appear overnight.

They are built over time.

The Strength to Stay

From what I've observed, couples who stay married for that long often have a certain level of determination about them.

At times it may even look like stubbornness.

But it's the kind of stubbornness that refuses to allow anything to break the vows they made.

They seem to carry a singular focus on honoring their commitment to one another.

That doesn't mean life is easy for them.

Every marriage faces challenges.

But the couples who make it through decades together appear to have made a decision early on that they will work through those challenges instead of walking away from them.

A Lifetime of Moments

When I imagine what marriage looks like after many decades, I hope love, respect, trust, and loyalty have all grown stronger over time.

I imagine two people who have seen the best and worst of life together.

Not just the polished moments captured in pictures.

But all the moments in between as well.

The difficult seasons.

The ordinary days.

The victories and the disappointments.

A lasting marriage isn't built only on the smiling moments captured in pictures.

It's built in all the moments that happen in between.

A Relationship That Stays Strong

When I picture growing old together, I hope the relationship itself is strong and healthy—much like a body that has been cared for over time.

In the same way that physical health requires attention and discipline, I believe a marriage must be cared for consistently over the years.

If it is nurtured properly, it can remain strong and thriving.

Showing up for each other year after year.

Season after season.

Built to Last

For a marriage to truly be built to last, priorities have to remain in order.

Intentions must stay clear and genuine.

Two people must continue moving in the same direction.

Their actions, goals, hopes, and dreams remain aligned with each other.

That kind of alignment doesn't happen by accident.

It requires effort, trust, and a continued commitment to the vows that started the journey in the first place.

Growing old together isn't simply about time passing.

It's about two people continuing to choose each other through every stage of life.

Closing Reflection

What I Hope to Learn

When I started writing this book, one of the first things I acknowledged was that I don't have marriage completely figured out.

That statement is still true.

Writing these chapters has reinforced how much there is still to learn.

Marriage is not something you master once and then move on from. It's something you grow into year after year.

There will always be new seasons, new challenges, and new opportunities to become a better husband.

What I Believe Matters Most

If there's one thing I feel confident about, it's that a strong marriage is built on staying connected—to God and to each other.

Faith provides direction and perspective.

When two people remain grounded in their relationship with God, it becomes easier to keep their priorities aligned with what truly matters.

And when spouses prioritize each other consistently, the marriage grows stronger over time.

That connection doesn't happen automatically.

It requires intention.

It requires effort.

And it requires the willingness to keep choosing your spouse even when life becomes busy or difficult.

What I'm Still Learning

Even after years of marriage, there are still areas where I'm trying to grow.

One of those areas is learning to communicate love in ways that resonate most with my wife.

My natural instinct has always been to show love through actions—through providing, serving, or giving.

But I've learned that what feels natural to me may not always be the clearest way for my wife to experience love.

So part of my growth as a husband is learning to speak her language.

Making sure she feels loved and valued in ways that matter to her, not just in the ways that come easiest to me.

Marriage requires that kind of awareness.

It requires the willingness to adjust and grow for the sake of the relationship.

Looking Ahead

When I think about the next twenty or thirty years, my hope is simple.

I hope my wife and I continue stacking good years on top of each other.

That doesn't mean life will always be easy.

There will be hard seasons.

There may be financial pressure, unexpected challenges, or moments that test our patience and resilience.

But my hope is that the things we value most remain at the center of our lives.

Faith.

Family.

Commitment.

And the daily decision to keep choosing each other.

If those priorities remain clear, the years ahead will continue building on the foundation we've already started.

What I Hope Readers Take Away

If someone finishes this book and takes away one idea, I hope it's this:

None of us have marriage completely figured out.

Not the author.

Not the reader.

Every couple makes mistakes.

Every couple faces difficult moments.

And every marriage requires grace—grace from God and grace from each other.

But honest, intentional effort goes a long way.

When two people are willing to work on their relationship, prioritize their spouse, and grow together over time, the marriage becomes stronger.

"Though one may be overpowered, two can defend themselves. A cord of three strands is not quickly broken."

— Ecclesiastes 4:12

Built to Last

In the end, a marriage that lasts isn't built on one big moment.

It's built through countless small choices made over many years.

A marriage that lasts is built by two people who stay in sync with God and with each other.

Two people who refuse to quit.

Who refuse to let the world pull them apart.

Who consistently honor, choose, protect, and fight for one another.

That kind of marriage doesn't happen overnight.

But when two people remain committed to the vows they made and the life they're building together, it becomes something worth striving for.

A marriage built to last.

About the Author

Kevin Horton is a husband, father, and business leader who believes the most important responsibilities in life happen at home.

Throughout his career, Kevin has held multiple leadership roles that have taken his family across several states. Those experiences have shaped his perspective on leadership, faith, family, and the importance of living with intention.

Kevin and his wife have built their life around faith, family, and the belief that strong homes create strong communities. Together they are raising their children with a focus on faith, discipline, and gratitude.

When he's not working or writing, Kevin enjoys spending time with his family, hunting, following Florida Gators athletics, and thinking about the next chapter of life.

Kevin writes about leadership, life lessons, faith, and personal growth with the goal of sharing practical insights that others can apply in their own lives.

For updates on future books, follow Kevin Horton on Amazon.

Other Books by Kevin Horton

Stewarded Influence

Faithful Leadership in a Performance-Driven World

A reflection on leadership, responsibility, and the importance of stewarding influence with integrity.

Raising Builders

A Father's Letters to His Sons on Faith, Discipline, and the Men God Intended Them to Become

A series of reflections and lessons from a father to his sons about faith, character, discipline, and becoming the kind of men God intended them to be.

Closer Than I Thought

Thirty Lessons I Learned in My Thirties

A collection of reflections on life, growth, priorities, and the lessons that often become clearer with age.

Financial Lessons I Wish I Knew

Avoid Costly Money Mistakes, Build Real Assets, and Achieve Financial Freedom

Practical lessons about money, stewardship, and long-term thinking learned through both mistakes and experience.